NATURE'S AMERICA

Published in the United States of America by
Roberts Rinehart Publishers
5455 Spine Road, Boulder, Colorado 80301

Distributed in the United States and Canada by Publishers Group West

Published in Ireland and the UK by
Roberts Rinehart Publishers
Trinity House, Charleston Road, Dublin 6, Ireland

International Standard Book Number 1-57098-024-1

Printed in China

DAVID MUENCH

NATURE'S AMERICA

TEXT BY
PATRICK O'DOWD

DESIGNED BY
BONNIE MUENCH

ROBERTS RINEHART PUBLISHERS

T O explore my responses to the world around me, to seek out the places on earth that seem unchanged since creation; these are central to my very existence. A need for the primal beauty in our landscape is for me a lifetime consuming search for identity.

The photographs in this portfolio are clues along this pathway, glimpses of place and image of my universe — a universe we all share together on this revolving earth.

The camera, and photographic process, serves the critical and important role of medium to these fleeting glimpses of my primal landscape — a landscape filled with natural rhythms, opposites, tolerances, mysteries, and clues. The camera (I use a large format 4 x 5) is the grand tool; it is used faithfully.

Looking from above in space everything is a cycle of light and shade, movement and stillness. Earth's revolving creates everywhere the illusion of sunrise and sunset. Winds circling and earth's shifts north and south bring us the seasonal cycle. Wet foggy rainforests; arid bony expanses of desert; and life giving salt marshes at ocean's edge, along with the complex buckling, heating, and cooling of the geologic forces, are all symbols of the original beauty I am compelled to work in. I hope for an enlightening contact with the primal world we came from. What is learned along the way is I find rare and precious.

Sensitive and perceptive photography can be conveyed in numerous ways; by metaphor; by symbol; or by transitory moments; or by essence (a direct perception of Nature's communication).

Working with transitory moments passing over the land has been my primary direction. These are the decisive moments Nature speaks to us of powerful changes brought about through milliniums of time. The first ray of warm sunlight after a brutal storm, the flicker of an ephemeral rainbow, great waterfalls on canyon walls after a heavy rain, etc., etc.

The essence of things perceived has always tugged at my photographing directions, although at the time hidden and submerged way down in my subconscious. Direct confrontation with the elemental forces of Nature is the ultimate challenge. To seek an essence of great forces of the unknown, to attempt affirmation and a harmony with these great forces is a never ending quest for the unattainable. Yet, I am optimistic.

The photographs in this portfolio hopefully will serve as reminders that a primal world does yet endure, although rapidly is diminishing because of Man's insensitive stewardship. I would be honored if my photographs serve as symbols for my children and their descendants of the strength and beauty of the land. For all the blessings granted to me I would hope to make this one contribution.

The energy most compelling in my work today attempts to bring a harmony to the opposite forces of a familiar raw power of the American West — expansive, dramatic, elemental — with that of a quieter, softer, more forgiving environment of the American East and Midwest —. Primal elements flourish in both. The same processes are occuring in each, but subject matter demands new approaches, patterns, and questions.

Where or what is this primal landscape I champion and seek identity in ? America abounds with a vast array of places to see and visit. Information is made endless by computer and booklets. Places I look for are usually related in some way to coastline, forest, alpine/mountain, desert, grassland, swamp/bog/marsh. Exposed rock, water (river and lake) are necessary additional ingredients.

Fortunately, and unique in America, great examples of these landforms are preserved in a very fine National Park system, both natural and historical, national monuments, national forests, wildlife refuges, state parks, and now very importantly significant wilderness areas. Some unusual examples are only preserved this way. Along with some recreation, all of these preserves hold a rare and precious gift, that of experiencing the pleasure of wild beauty from some undisturbed landscape.

Aside from being an introspective artform, photography is communication for my real work. Whether the photographs are considered "Art" is not as important. What is more important is reaching into the past for a place in the continuum of time and thought. To capture a certain moment in time on film is undeniably exhilirating; but searching my responses to the moment and place, are so seductive and attracting. The questions asked render answers so revealing about ourselves... a pure communication with the environment may be ?

David Muench
Santa Barbara
1984

LIKE Benjamin Franklin who one day when out riding with friends couldn't resist the compulsion to charge down a hill toward a fierce whirlwind he had spied and probe and touch it with his horsewhip (nor tickling clouds with kites and keys in search of mysterious electrical essences), so David Muench can't resist roaming America in search of its essence — a mysterious something behind light and shadow, experience and his photographs.

Nature's America is the first time David Muench has put an order to his forty year quest for the secret heart of America and its people. In doing so, he has posed the ancient conundrum for both Americans and their European observers — What is an American ?

It is natural that he should do this. The son of a well-known german-american photographer, he is looking for his own roots. Our great fortune and pleasure is that the fruits of his research, here presented, make David Muench, America's pre-eminent living landscape photographer. He has been to the sacred places and recorded their voice in light and shadow. Nature has spoken and even sung for David Muench and the songs are here recorded for you to see and feel.

Like so many, whether they be historians, poets, politicians, itinerant travel writers, or a host of others, David Muench has found that the essence of American character was the result of the struggle between transplanted peoples and the American land. This is not a new idea. As early as 1782, J. Hector St. Jean de Crevecœur in *Letters from an American Farmer,* first published in London, was explaining to his fellow Europeans that the land explains America.

« Men are like plants: the goodness and flavor of the fruit proceeds from the peculiar soil and exposition in which they grow. We are nothing but what we derive from the air we breathe, the climate we inhabit, the government we obey, the system of religion we profess... »

But the most classic and enduring exposition of this idea was given by the historian Frederick Jackson Turner in 1893. He had read some census reports that announced the closing of the area of free land in the United States. As a boy, Turner loved the virgin forest and thrilled on seeing deer in the river — antlered beauties who watched him come down with curious eyes and then broke for the tall timber. He remembered squaws in the village on the high bank, talking their low treble to the bass of Indian polesmen on the river. He had a feeling that he belonged to all that and to read that all this was ending was a serious fact with important consequences for American destiny. He wrote that

« The existence of an area of free land... explains American development... The wilderness masters the colonist. It finds him a European in dress, industries, tools, modes of travel and thought. It takes him from the railroad car and puts him in the birch canoe. It strips off the garments of civilization and arrays him in the hunting shirt and the moccasin. It puts him in the log cabin of the Cherokee and Iroquois and runs an Indian palisade around him... The outcome is a new product that is, American. »

For Turner, the struggle with the wilderness created American democracy, nationalism, mobility, restlessness, ingenuity, and all the other so-called American traits. For him, the disappearence of free or cheap land would bode ill for the American republic.

Others too, but much earlier had found contact with the land vital to American destiny. One of them, Thomas Jefferson extolled the virtues of the yeoman farmer. He thought that the American environment was what made America great and was the guarantor of its future even if history had shown that all previous governments had decayed into tyranny and despotism. Such had been the case of Republican Rome and Britain's cherished Anglo-Saxon liberties. But American government would be guaranteed by the virtue of its people whose close contact with nature nourished a virtuous ways of life, securing dignity, competency, and independence, the essential characteristics necessary to support free government. Jefferson loved the yeoman farmer.

« Corruption of morals in the mass of cultivators is a phenomenon of which no age nor nation has furnished an example ... those who labor in the earth are the chosen people of God, if ever He had a chosen people whose breasts he had made his peculiar deposit for substantial and genuine virtue. It is the focus in which He keeps alive that sacred fire, which otherwise might escape from the face of the earth. »

Contact with nature would save us, wrote Jefferson. And what of the origin of evil ? It was as easily explained; it was the conjunction of vice and industry.

« Corruption of morals is the mark set on those, who not looking up to heaven; to their own toil and industry as does the husbandman for their subsistence, depend for it on the casualties and caprices of customers. Dependence begets subservience and venality, suffocates the germs of virtue, and prepares fit tools for the designs of ambition... the proportion which the aggregate of the other classes bears in any State to that of its husbandman, is the proportion of *its unsound* to its healthy parts, and is a good enough barameter whereby to measure its degree of corruption. While we have land to labor then, let us never wish to see our citizens occupied at a work-bench or twirling a distaff. »

For Jefferson, only contact with the American land could provide the necessary regenerative force to guarantee virtue in the republic.

David Muench has given us a glimpse of what the American world was like in the beginning. It must have been incredible. We know from early explorer's accounts and ship's logs that one could smell and sense the rich abundance of the primeval American forest more than 200 miles at sea. But Nature's imprint on the first hardy Puritan and Pilgrim settlements — the first groups to seriously colonize (they brought their women with them), was not rapture but naked fear. As the governor of the Plymouth Colony, William Bradford, wrote in 1634 ten years after their arrival:

But here I cannot but stay and make a pause, and stand half amazed at this poor people's present condition; and so I think will the reader too, when he well considers the same. Being thus passed the vast ocean, and a sea of troubles before in their preparations, they had now no friends to welcome them, nor inns to entertain or refresh their weatherbeaten bodies, no houses or much less towns to repair to, to seek for succor. It is recorded in scripture as a mercy to the apostle and his shipwrecked company, that the barbarians showed them no small kindness in refreshing them, but these savage barbarians, when they met with them were readier to fill their sides full of arrows then otherwise. And for the season it was winter, and they that know the winters of that country know them to be sharp and violent, and subject to cruel and fierce storms, dangerous to travel to known places, much more to search for an unknown coast. Besides, what could they see but a hidious and desolate wilderness, full of wild beasts and wild men ? »

So armed with but faith, these « strona men with empire in their brains », so celebrated in American history, responded to the harshness of those hard early days by building sturdy settlements and townships and founding traditions of hard work, education, and science and all the other characteristics that have brought America to greatness. For the early founders were armed with the idea that they were a special people — an Elect; a nation upon whom, from the beginning, the hand of God has peculiarly been placed. As a 17th century Puritan explained it, « we are a special seed winnowed from the chaff of the Old World to work God's will on Earth ». A very demanding destiny, don't you think ? But harsh nature can build strong men.

Most European looking toward America dismiss American achievement because of our youngness. The idea is an old one. As the Abbé Reynal wrote in the 18th century, going west would only condemn transplanted Europeans to waste and decay in a wretched New World. He formulated the belittling and stinging observation that « America had not produced one good poet, one talented mathematician, or one man of genius in a single art or a single science ». We have been on the cultural defensive ever since. The story says we have no past. We are too young.

I remember the comment when I was teaching in France. « What do you do ? » said a Frenchman.

« I teach American Cultural History ». I answered.

« Must be a short course », he replied. And so it goes.

But there are other ways of looking at this question and the natural world captured by David Muench suggests the response. Nature's America expresses her ancientness with redwood trees over 3000 years old, bristlecone pines even older, or the grand canyon cutting through billions of years of geologic time.

Or one might consider our true ancient civilizations. Thomas Jefferson believed that one tribe was linked to a lost tribe of Israel. He studied their language and weights and measures and found relations to Roman science. But it isn't necessary to explain it, the images of David Muench tell us. Truly great and profound civilizations existed in ancient America — civilizations whose kivas tell of their connectedness with the earth and whose architecture so perfectly fits the land.

Perhaps the right response for us is Gertrude Stein's observation that America is the oldest country in the 20th century. Founded at the beginning of the modern era, no other country has such long modern traditions.

For David Muench as for most Americans, Nature is a manifestation of God's plan. This imbues his study of nature with the incredible depth of feeling that is evident in his photographs. He has accomplished this through a genuine love and understanding of the elements of nature. He speaks of bony deserts, nourishing oceans and sees all Nature as alive. In the gradations of light fixed forever on his photographic negatives, there is always the mysterious light and rigidity of natural form all linked by an inobtrusive artist and finished with silence and repose.

His art comes out of Nature and he scrupulously accepts whatever she presents. He turns to Nature to learn his alphabet — the ways a weed grows, the life history of a tree as evidenced the conformations of its limbs, the effects of atmosphere on light and color, the mathematical ratios of light on water. By studying nature with such intensity, he has increased his power of sight and his ability to define form. David Muench is a seer. And even more important, he has developed his capacity for love, love that grew with knowledge, seeing what was there exactly for what it was without artifice or false sentiment. In the end, David Muench leaves us with harmony.

The American land has formed the American character and its vast spaces have also provided a safety valve for the restless and discontented among us. The tale says that Daniel Boone would always move westward whenever he saw smoke from another man's cabin. With all that space the land has saved us from the revolutions and wars that have marked the lives of other nations. The land's heritage has been our optimism about what is just over the next ridge, in the next valley. The momentum and vitality of that spirit has continued as Americans go outward toward new frontiers — the stars and beyond, always sure that God's plan will be revealed to them and that their destiny will give law unto the world. May that they understand Nature's America and not America's Nature.

At the time of the creation of the United States, Tom Paine's best seller, *Common Sense,* proclaimed that

« We have it in our power to begin the world over again. A situation similar to the present has not happened since the days of Noah until now. »

And the writer of the *Declaration of Independence* which was written to explain to the world our reasoning, declared it was our « self-evident right, and a sacred duty to the Law's of Nature and Nature's God » to become a Nation. May America once again renew herself and « learn from the green world what can be thy place ».

Patrick O'Dowd
Santa Barbara
1984

PRIMEVAL

"Thus, in the beginning, all the world was America."

John Locke
Seventeenth Century

Cinder cone. Lassen National Park, California.

Haleakala National Park, Hawaii.

Sequoia National Park, California.

Sunrise. Galveston Island State Park, Texas.

Big Sur Coastline, California.

Cape Arago, Oregon.

Allegheny National Forest, Pennsylvania.

Autumn swamp. Woods Bay State Park, South Carolina.

Bald Cypress. Reelfoot Lake, Tennessee.

Pyramid Lake, Nevada.

Green River Overlook. Canyonlands National Park, Utah.

Painted Desert, Arizona.

Cacti. Lake Mead, Arizona.

La Moille Canyon. Ruby Mountains, Nevada.

Columbine. Yankee Boy Basin, Colorado.

Adirondack Mountains, New York.

Linville Falls. Blue Ridge Parkway, North Carolina.

Rhododendron. Redwood National Park, California.

Hoh Rainforest. Olympic National Park, Washington.

Bandon Beach, Oregon.

ANTIQUITY

In beauty, I walk
Beauty before me, I walk
Beauty above me, I walk
Beauty below me, I walk

In beauty, I walk
To the direction of the rising sun,
in beauty, I walk
To the direction traveling with the sun,
in beauty, I walk
To the direction of the setting sun,
in beauty, I walk
To the direction of the dippers,
in beauty, I walk

All around me my land is beauty,
In beauty, I walk.

Navajo Yebechei Chant

Anasazi Petroglyph. San Francisco Peaks, Arizona

Sequoia National Park, California.

Ancient Bristlecone Pines. White Mountains, California.

Long Logs. Petrified Forest National Park, Arizona.

Ancient Bristlecone Pine. White Mountains, California.

Grand Canyon National Park, Arizona.

Acoma Pueblo, New Mexico.

Colorado River. Grand Canyon National Park, Arizona.

Pueblo Bonito. Chaco Culture National Historical Park, New Mexico.

Taos Pueblo, New Mexico.

White House ruin. Canyon de Chelly National Monument, Arizona.

Pictographs. Canyonlands National Park, Utah.

Petroglyphs. Nine Mile Canyon, Utah.

Inscription House, Navajo National Monument, Arizona.

Mug House ruin and kiva. Mesa Verde National Park, Colorado.

Canyon de Chelly National Monument, Arizona.

White House ruin, Canyon de Chelly National Monument, Arizona.

LIGHT

"Standing on the bare ground,
—my head bathed by the blithe air,
and uplifted into infinite space,
—all mean egotism vanishes.
I become a transparent eyeball ;
I am nothing ; I see all ;
the currents of the Universal Being circulate through me ;
I am part or parcel of God"

Ralph Waldo Emerson
1836

White Sands National Monument, New Mexico.

Tideland Marsh. Cedar Point, North Carolina.

Watercress. Zion National Park, Utah.

Delicate Arch. Arches National Park, Utah.

North Window. Arches National Park, Utah.

Biscuit Geyser Basin. Yellowstone National Park, Wyoming.

Lodgepole Pines. Yellowstone National Park, Wyoming.

El Capitan. Yosemite National Park, California.

Snowmass Canyon, Colorado.

Colorado River. Deadhorse Point State Park, Utah.

Comb Reef, Utah.

Mitten Rocks. Monument Valley Tribal Park, Utah-Arizona.

Toroweap. Grand Canyon National Park, Arizona.

Pinaleno Mountains, Arizona.

White Mesa Arch, Arizona.

Lake Powell, Arizona.

Black Rock Desert, Nevada.

Seastacks. Cannon Beach, Oregon.

FORM

"Natural things were ordered for types of spiritual things."

Jonathan Edwards
Eighteenth Century

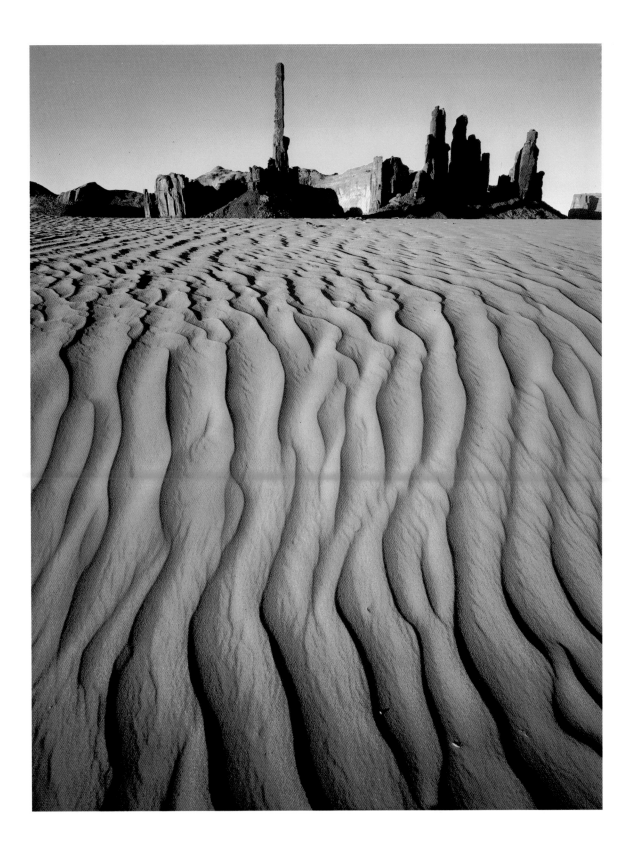

Yebechei Rocks. Monument Valley Navajo Tribal Park, Arizona.

Echo Canyon. Zion National Park, Utah.

Metamorphics. Santa Catalina Mountains, Arizona.

Mount Hayden. Grand Canyon National Park, Arizona.

Mesquite Flat Dunes. Death Valley National Monument, California.

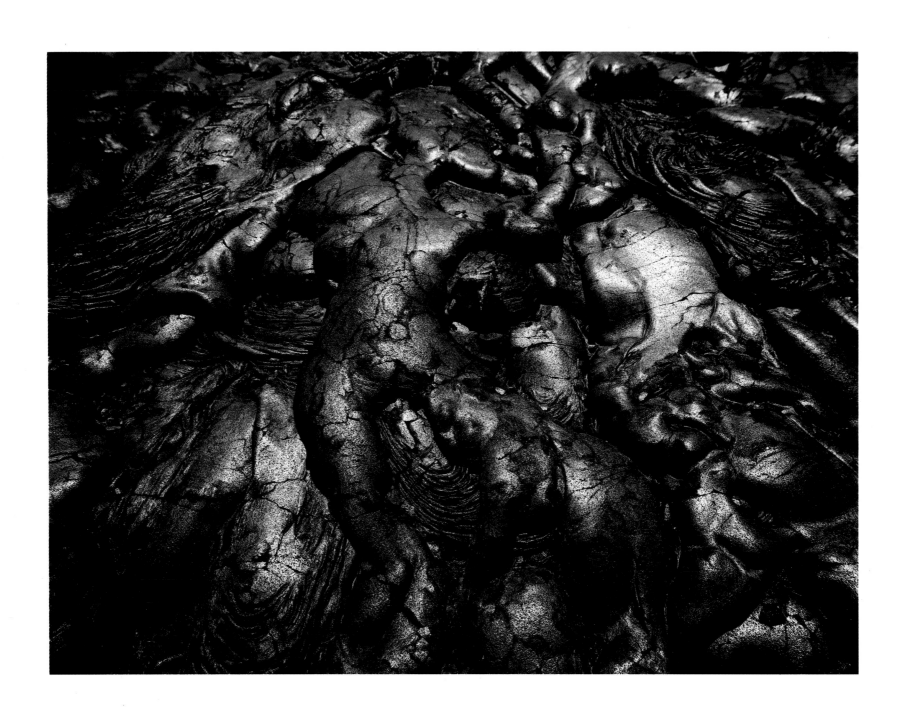

Pahoehoe Lava. Hawaii Volcanoes National Park, Hawaii.

Bristlecone pine skeleton. Mount Hamilton, Nevada.

Point Lobos State Reserve, California.

Santa Cruz Coastline, California.

Pemigewasset Stream. Franconia Notch, New Hampshire.

Green River Overlook. Canyonlands National Park, Utah.

Mount Whitney. Sierra Nevada Range, California.

Maple. Whidbey Island, Washington.

Sierra Juniper. Carson Pass, Sierra Nevada Range, California.

Mesquite Flat Dunes. Death Valley National Monument, California.

Yucca. White Sands National Monument, New Mexico.

Great Sand Dunes National Monument, Colorado.

Henry Mountains, Utah.

Bryce Canyon National Park, Utah.

Rainbow Bridge National Monument, Utah.

Natural Bridge. Canyonlands National Park, Utah.

SPACE

" The existence of an area of free land... explains American development. ... The wilderness masters the colonist. It finds him a European in dress, industries, tools, modes of travel, and thought. It takes him from the railroad car and puts him in the birch canoe. It strips off the garments of civilization and arrays him in the hunting shirt and the moccasin. It puts him in the log cabin of the Cherokee and Iroquois and runs an Indian palisade around him... the outcome... is a new product that is American."

Frederick Jackson Turner
1893

Table Mesa, New Mexico.

Grand Canyon National Park, Arizona.

Mount Washington, New Hampshire.

Standing Rock Basin. Canyonlands National Park, Utah.

Monument Basin. Canyonlands National Park, Utah.

Badwater. Death Valley National Monument, California.

Dantes View. Death Valley National Monument, California.

Saquaro cacti. Baboquivari Peak, Arizona.

Agave stalks. Santa Rita Mountains, Arizona.

Shiprock, New Mexico.

Vermillion Cliffs. Colorado River, Arizona.

Grasslands. Agate Fossil Beds National Monument, Nebraska.

Owens Lake. Mohave Desert, California.

Cape Canaveral National Seashore, Florida.

Santa Elena Canyon. Big Bend National Park, Texas.

Eunice Lake. **Mount** Rainier National Park, Washington.

Waterlillies. San Juan Mountains, Colorado.

Second Beach. Olympic National Park, Washington.

Ecola State Park, Oregon.

Snake River beaver pond. Grand Teton National Park, Wyoming.

MOTION

"Every year 40 million Americans change their residence."

Recent American Census Report

"In Europe people talk a great deal of the wilds of America, but the Americans themselves never think about them. Their eyes are fixed upon another sight, they march across these wilds, draining swamps, turning the course of rivers, peopling solitudes, and subduing nature."

Alexis de Tocqueville
1832

Latir Creek. Sangre de Cristo Range, New Mexico.

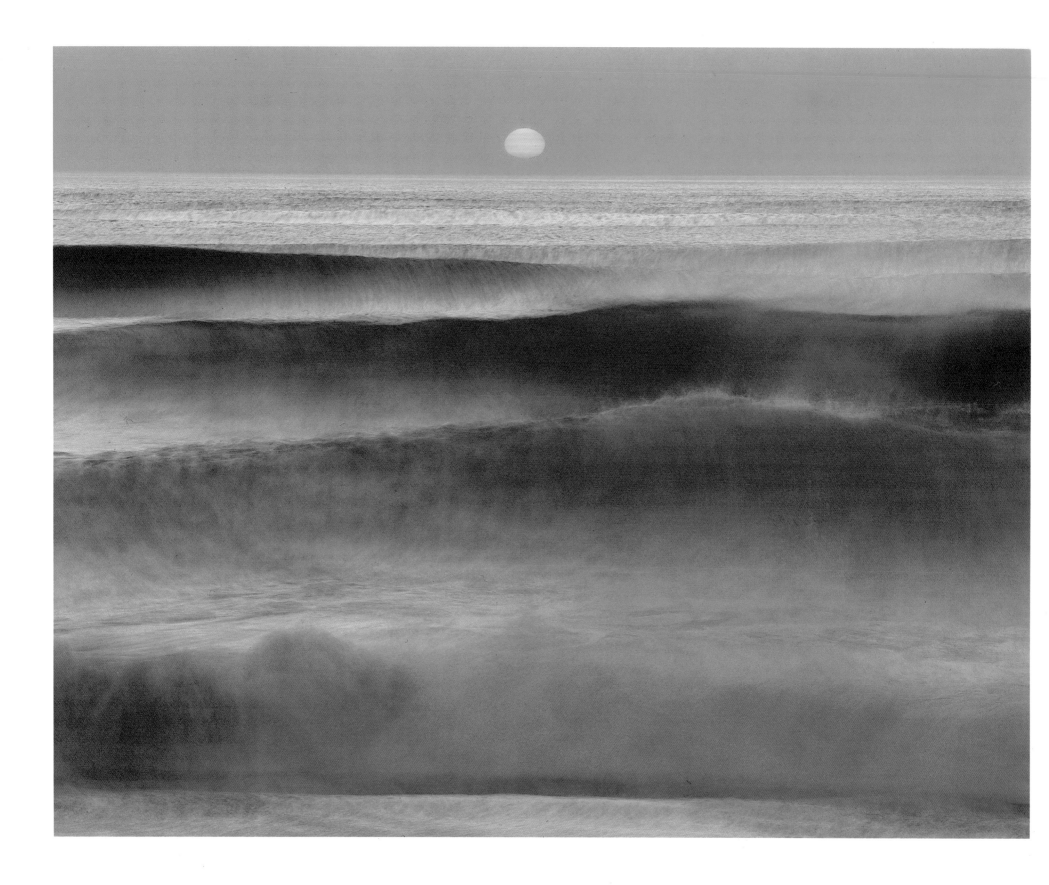

Cape Cod National Seashore, Massachusetts.

Big Sur Coastline, California

Del Norte Coastline, Redwoods National Park, California.

Eagle Falls. Lake Tahoe, California.

Eagle Creek Punchbowl, Oregon.

Roaring Fork. Aspen, Colorado.

Havasu Falls. Grand Canyon National Park, Arizona.

Deer Creek Gorge. Grand Canyon National Park, Arizona.

Lower Falls of the Yellowstone. Yellowstone National Park, Wyoming.

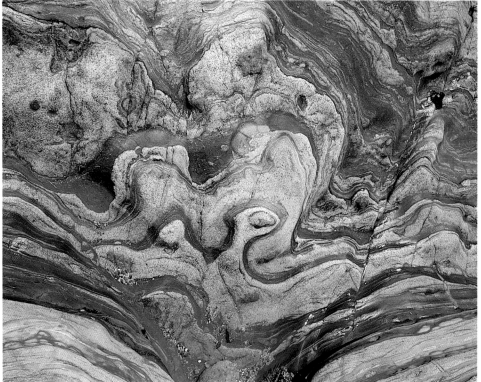

Garapatta. Big Sur Coastline, California.

Sandstone forms. Point Lobos State Reserve, California.

Bristlecone Pine. Mount Hamilton, Nevada.

Kent Falls. Hausatonic River, Connecticut.

Hungry Creek. Bitterroot Range, Idaho.

Cobble mosaic. Mc Donald Creek. Glacier National Park, Montana.

RENEWAL

"What thou lovest well is thy true heritage
What thou lov'st well shall not be reft from thee.
The ant's a centaur in his dragon world.
Pull down thy vanity, it is not man
Made courage, or made order, or made grace,
Pull down thy vanity, I say pull down.
Learn of the green world what can be thy place
In scaled invention or true artistry,
Pull down thy vanity,
Paquin pull down !
The green casque has outdone your elegance".

Ezra Pound
The Pisan Cantos
Twentieth Century

Paintbrush and Bluebonnet. Hill Country, Texas.

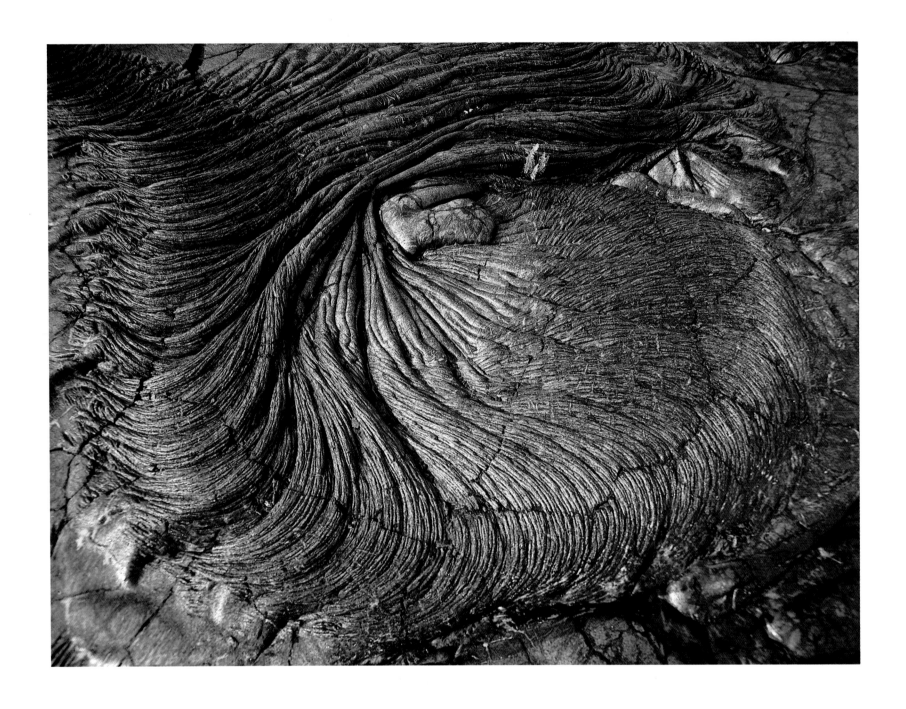

Lava. Hawaii Volcanoes National Park, Hawaii.

Buckweat bloom. San Francisco Peaks, Arizona.

Bristlecone pine. Windy Ridge, Colorado.

Paintbrush and upturned roots. Mosquito Range, Colorado.

Del Norte Redwoods. Redwood National Park, California.

Forest floor. Cape Disappointment, Washington.

Mount Greylock, Massachusetts.

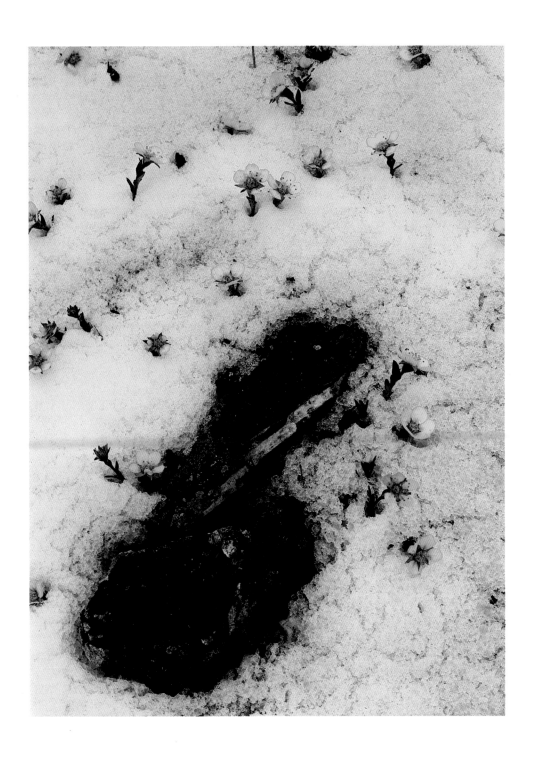

Saxifrage bloom in July snow. San Juan Range, Colorado.

144 Hardwood forest. Concord, Massachusetts.

Hearts Content preserve. Allegheny National Forest, Pennsylvania.

Lupine spread. Jarbidge Mountains, Nevada.

Primrose and Paintbrush. Hill Country, Texas.

Eastern Dogwood. Kings Mountain, South Carolina.

Maple leaves. Androscogin River Valley, New Hampshire.   149

Hedgehog and cholla cacti. Anza Borrego Desert State Park, California.

Kofa Mountains, Arizona.

Elephant tree and Palms. Anza Borrego Desert State Park, California.

Aspen boles. Coconino National Forest, Arizona.

Gold poppy. Sonoran Desert, Arizona.